High Energy Secrets

By Joe Apfelbaum

How I lost over 95 pounds, kept it off, and have higher energy levels than ever!

Joe Apfelbaum

APFELBAUM

Contact Joe
Apfelbaum via his
website:
www.joeapfelbaum.com

Connect on social media and reach out!

Produced in the United States of America

Dedication:

This book is dedicated to all those who are on their journey to a better life. Congratulations on taking the first step to improving your energy levels and for allowing me to share my journey with you.

Thank you to all my friends on social media who encouraged me while I shared my journey over the years.

Thank you for those first 10 'likes' from my Facebook friends, who got me moving and taking action.

Thank you to those who helped me in editing this book and for your feedback and comments.

Endorsements:

"Joe has a 'method to his madness', and most importantly it leads to results. Joe is not afraid to put himself out there for the benefit of others, and this book is another example of that. Joe shares how he maintains a high energy level --every day, and how he lost almost 100 pounds... right before our eyes! Whether you see him on Facebook or have never heard of him before, this book will provide you valuable insight on your road to success and happiness."

- David Schnurman, CEO Lawline

"I watched Joe on Instagram discuss his weight-loss journey and I took action. Within 3 months I lost 25 pounds and I feel healthier and higher energy than ever!" - An anonymous young man I met that told me that he saw my instagram and was so proud that he took action and got results.

Introduction

People often ask me, "Joe, where do you get all this energy from? Energy to run a multi-million dollar business, energy to manage your family life, and *still* have enough energy to write books and coach entrepreneurs on how to take their lives to the next level?"

I feel very lucky to be able to have all this energy, power and freedom in my life. I am very grateful that I found ways to create vitality in my life. It was not always this way.

It's true, I remember not long ago, when I would work 16 hours a day and my energy was extremely low for the majority of the day... and I did not understand why!

I constantly searched for answers; something to help me get through my day. I knew that when I drank a Snapple, I would feel better, but within an hour, I would crash again. I tried smoking, eating different foods, and anything I could think of that would change my condition, without having to put in too much effort.

In my mind, exercise was not an option, because I did not have "time" and it was "hard work". Salads were for "ladies" and veggies for "wimps". Obviously, I had a serious mindset problem.

I wanted to enjoy "real food" - steak and burgers, french fries and fried chicken! I don't know where I got that mindset from because growing up, I ate salad all the time and my parents did not teach me to focus on the worst possible foods.

I realize now that I was missing awareness, strategy and accountability. This is the reason that I am writing this book. So I can help the people out there that want and need higher levels of energy with the methods that I used.

It's 5:38 am as I write this sentence, and I'm getting ready to have an amazing day! Right in front of me, I have a tall cup of cold water and my exercise gear, ready to go for a nice 3 mile run, in the crisp 60 degree weather in Brooklyn, N.Y.

My life has changed dramatically over the past few years. I went from being tired, lethargic and incredibly overweight, to becoming a person who is happier, has more energy and feels good in his mind and body. I am able to do so much more with my day now.

I can't remember the last time I got a cold, or felt sick. I now understand why people get sick and how to prevent those feelings in my own body.

My goal is to keep this book at 90 pages, so you can read this book over the course of a weekend -- or you can read a page a day, for 90 days.

I am not a big fan of fluff, so I will be providing you with practical tips that you can use right away, after you've consulted with your medical advisor first, of course.

Let's go on this journey together!

www.joeapfelbaum.com

You have the power to change your life. The first step is to decide that you are ready to begin your journey!

- Joe Apfelbaum

Table of Contents

"The Right Energy Will Save You A Decade."

- Joe Apfelbaum

How I Got Started On My Journey To Lose 90 Pounds

There I was, sitting on my couch taking a video of my children with my cell phone. The kids were having a blast, running around, dancing, giggling and being themselves. After a few minutes, I stopped taking the video and we all gathered around my phone to watch it.

There was a heaving sound in the background and I could not make out what the noise was. I asked my wife what that sound was, and she said, "Oh, that's you breathing!"

How could that be me? It sounded like an elephant trying to get out of a plastic tube of toothpaste.

That is how I felt, because I was 265 pounds and I was in denial about my weight. I gained 90 pounds from age 23 to 33 by ignoring my health. I only focused on my business, I did not value exercise, I did not value nutrition. I remember buying cases of Snapple from Costco and drinking about 6 bottles a day. How refreshing it was to hear the snap of the cap and look under to read the fact, smiling while holding it with my chubby fingers.

Each year my waist would get wider, until a size 42 waist started feeling tight. For the first time, I had to purchase pants with an elastic waist, and I can still remember how relieved, yet embarrassed, I felt.

I never really looked at myself in the mirror. Did my looks really matter? My one priority was all I wanted: to be financially secure. Stay focused on business and everything else will work out.

Joe Apfelbaum

There were many excuses that I made about my weight issues. I remember thinking, if I lose weight, I might lose my personality. If I lose all this weight, I won't be happy anymore. This is just who I am, I need to learn to accept it. I love food and I just need to work really hard and keep making money.

Asking For Help

I asked my wife to help me lose weight and she looked at me and said the hard truth: "You have to be willing to do the work, it has to come from you!"

Then I turned to my friends to see if they could help me lose weight. We got together at a restaurant to discuss ideas. After enjoying a few appetizers, a massive main dish and some dessert, I realized they probably would not be able to help me.

It was not about the numbers for me. It was about being healthy and having enough energy to impact the world. My doctor told me that If I didn't lose the weight, I would end up getting diabetes and would be at risk for many other diseases that come from unhealthy food choices and not moving enough.

One evening, after going to a restaurant and overeating yet again, I was double-parked outside my house and waiting for a spot. Parking is hard to find on my block in Brooklyn and I did not want to park too far away because I didn't want to have to walk. After waiting 15 minutes I realized that no one was moving, so I was left with no choice but to go look for a spot a few blocks away.

I found a spot three blocks away and as I was waiting to cross the parkway, I looked at my phone and noticed that my social media had no notifications.

High Energy Secrets

If I have a few hundred friends on Facebook but no engagement, are they really friends? The people closest to me were not able to help me lose weight. Maybe some of these "friends" can help me. So in a final desperate wave of helplessness, I posted on Facebook. I took a social risk, communicating that I needed help, and pledged to walk one minute per like. I had finally confessed, in public, that I needed help.

I went to sleep with the expectation that no one would respond to my plea for help, thinking that it was a joke.

When I woke up and checked my phone, I noticed that 10 people had liked the post. I could not believe that my little post got ten people to take action. This was a huge motivation for me.

I went for a 10 minute walk/jog and posted a photo and video of myself, to prove to my Facebook friends that I actually did it.

The next day, I posted again, telling people I would go on a bike ride, one minute per like. Wow! I got 20 likes. I was on to something. Now, I finally had motivation to get moving.

Why This Worked

Attention has always been my drug, and when I used my need for attention to set my goal, it worked. I was getting dozens of hits of dopamine each day from all the people that were watching and engaging with me.

Before I knew it, I was getting about 70 likes a day and I was jogging about 7 miles. Needless to say, I lost about 37 pounds in the first year of using this method and I signed up for my first half marathon.

After reading over a dozen books and speaking to a few dozen people about their weight loss journeys, I realized that weight loss is one of the biggest challenges people face in their lifetime.

It's more about food than it is about exercise, but the combination is key to keep moving forward. Staying away from the wrong foods by changing my relationship with food was the other factor for me.

Over the past few years, I have lost over 90 pounds and I found new freedom and new purpose. I have inspired the people closest to me to lose weight and change their lives for the better. Every time someone sees the new me, they are reminded that I changed my life for the better by taking control of my poor eating habits and changing how I look at exercise.

By reading this book "High Energy Secrets" you will learn what I did, and what you can do too, to gain control over your health. It's not about another diet or fad to get you to lose weight fast. It's about understanding why some people are healthy and some people are not and what you can do if you want to take control of your health.

Let's get into our minds first and after that we will review some practical tips to get you going!

High Energy Mindset - The Two Minds

We each have two minds; the conscious mind and the subconscious mind. There is a constant battle of control between these two forces that happens in our lives. We call the battle "self-control".

When we see someone exercising self control, what is actually happening is that they are using their conscious mind to control their subconscious mind.

Think about this for a moment. Are you breathing right now? Are you aware of your breath every time you take a breath or does it 'just happen' for you?

Are you breathing deeply or are you taking shallow breaths?

Stop and take a very deep breath by filling your belly through your nose and slowly blowing it out of your mouth.

If you have a baby near you, blow the air onto their face and see what happens. I love blowing air into my baby's face to see the delight she gets when my breath tickles her face. Just keep in mind that if they start crying you might want to consider brushing your teeth. (JK!)

You just controlled your breath with your conscious mind and you affected the subconscious of your baby by getting an automatic reaction out of the baby by blowing in the baby's face.

I found that it was very exhausting and energy depleting to keep using my conscious mind and exercising self control in order to eat the right foods. We have a limited amount of willpower. I did not understand that my choices were being made automatically, without my input, when I ate the entire bag of onion garlic potato chips as a snack before my fast food rampage at Kosher Delight.

Walk into the grocery store and think to yourself, "I need something really tasty," and see where you go automatically. Don't think about it, just go and see where your body will take you. Mine used to take me to the snack aisle. Now it takes me to the nuts section.

It's not your fault, so do not blame yourself for possessing the habits that you have today. Most of your habits were given to you as an unwanted and unasked for gift. I am sure you have heard that every time you do something that causes you to feel pleasure, you create a pathway in your brain. The more often you do that activity and get pleasure, the stronger the pathway becomes.

When I weighed 265 pounds, I had very strong mental pathways for eating Kaiser rolls with cream cheese, lettuce, tomato, and a pickle with a tall glass of Tropicana orange juice as a snack before my massive cheese omelette was finished cooking.

I used to feel guilty that I was majorly overweight and that guilt and shame would send me back to seek more comfort foods like a box of Joyva jelly rings. You read that correctly, an entire box!

The first step to gaining control of your energy is to understand your mind. If you get what needs to be done to your mind, the rest of this book, the strategies and practical advice, will be easily implemented. Without the mindset piece, change won't be likely.

80% of your results come from your mindset and only 20% come from your skillset. If you feel ashamed, guilty, depressed or angry, you will not be able to learn the skills you need to take action.

The first step of the popular 12 step program for addictions is to acknowledge that you are powerless. When you realize that your subconscious mind runs the show most of the day, you will start to see that you really are powerless and the results you've gotten until now were automatic.

That might depress you at first, but realize that if it's all software and therefore, automatic. All you need to do is hack the software and you will get it to perform how you want.

Hacking the software takes hard work and persistence. It will be easy to give up and continue to do the same old, same old, but if you take one piece of 'code' at a time and hack it with the secrets I will show you, you will change your energy levels forever. Let's begin by setting some goals and figuring out why we even want to go on this high energy journey to begin with.

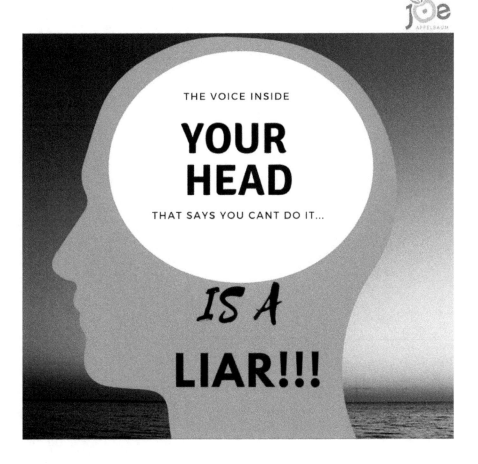

Joe Apfelbaum

What Habits Do You Have Right Now That You Want To Rewire?

_____

_____

_____

_____

_____

_____

How To Set Health Goals That Work

When I ask business owners and entrepreneurs how much money they want to make in their business, most tell me the same thing: "I want to make as much as possible."

I usually laugh because I used to think that way before I had the courage to pick a specific number. A number that, at first glance, I thought limited my potential but was actually very realistic and attainable. Any number seems like a small number when thoughts like "I want more! I want it all right away! Why would I want to limit myself?" would crowd my head.

When I was in the 8th grade, a teacher I didn't really respect, took me to the office, sat me down, and told me that the most important thing in life was to set goals.

"What do you want to do with your life? Who do you want to become?" the teacher asked me. I thought to myself, "I would like to set a goal to get out of this office and never see you again!"

Clearly, I was never a person who valued setting goals, yet, now I am so goal-oriented. I talk about goals every day with clients, employees, and family members. I discuss strategies to get to my goals and to help other people get to their goals.

Most people have vague goals. I call those types of goals wishes.

A goal without a timeline is a wish.

Wishing you were better will not make you better. You must figure out what "better" specifically means and set smart goals.

SMART is an acronym for:
Specific and **S**imple

Measurable and **M**ojovational
Attainable and **A**ctionable
Relevant and **R**ealistic
Timebound and **T**oday-centric.

When you set a smart goal that is specific, you gain the ability to get excited.

Most people are not motivated to lose weight because they have not taken the time to set a smart goal.

An Unmotivated Person might say, "I really should lose weight. After the holidays I will lose tons of weight and be fit again. I am setting a goal to take charge of my health for once and for all. My goal is to lose 100 pounds in the next month and keep it off, finally!"

That is not motivating to me. It sounds like something that is hard to do and not realistic. Instead, let's look at another goal.

Motivated Person: "I must lose weight. On, Monday, Dec 31st I will weigh 199 pounds. I will lose 16 pounds by that date and that will make me feel amazing. I am setting a goal to drink 100 ounces of water each day, 8 ounces per hour for 12 hours. I will prepare 3 preplanned meals each weekday and I will give myself a cheat meal on the weekends. I will measure my progress daily for the next 90 days starting TODAY. Now someone get me a glass of water!"

Do you understand the difference between a person who wants to get rich quick, and a person who sets a small, measurable, attainable, actionable goal that is realistic, within a real time frame?

The key is to gain momentum. Once we have momentum we start to feel the progress in our lives and then we are motivated to create more progress. So, set a smaller goal and actually achieve it, so that you can get a taste of what it means to have success.

Before we set a goal we need to take a moment to understand the reason for setting goals.

"Energy without strategy is a waste of time."

- Joe Apfelbaum

Why Set a Goal If You Don't Understand Why You Want To Get To The Goal?

If your goal does not excite you, you will not take action.

Excitement comes from motivation and motivation comes from the word "Motive".

Feelings come from reasons.

We are driven by our "Why". The more powerful our "Why," the more powerful the feelings that compel us to take action will become.

Why do you want more energy? What is your motive? Do you have a good reason?

My kids always ask me WHY they should do what I told them to do. If I just say, "cause Daddy said so," they are not so compelled. But, instead, if I find a reason and I embed that reason in my request, they get excited and motivated to take action.

It might not be the best parenting advice because you don't want your kids to just do things for a good reason, but, for me personally, it works when the kids are tired and I need them to take action.

Unmotivational Request: "Kids go take a shower and put on your PJs, bedtime is in just one hour." 10 minutes later. "Kids go take a shower and put on your PJs, bedtime is in just 50 minutes." 10 minutes later. "Kids go take a shower and put on your PJs, bedtime is in just 40 minutes." You get where this is going?

Instead, think about how reason and motivation come into play.

Motivational Request: "Kids, who wants to watch an amazing funny cartoon with Daddy on his phone and have a yummy treat?" I hear yelling "Me!" I continue. "We have only one hour till bedtime and the show starts in 20 minutes, you all need to be showered and in PJ's to be able to watch the show and get the treat. Whoever is ready first gets to hold the phone!" 20 minutes later they are all in PJs trying to win the race to be first.

They still need reminding and the same reason won't work for each kid. In addition, the reason needs to change each time to be effective, as kids keep getting older and wiser. If you don't have a good reason, you won't really get good results.

Ask yourself why you want to get healthy, or, why you want to have great energy.

I want to run around with my kids, I want to be able to train 10,000 entrepreneurs each year to take charge of their business, family, and self. I want to feel incredible each morning and keep finding a better way to take my life to the next level.

What is your reason?

_____
_____
_____

What is your SMART Goal?

_____
_____

When I coach people we set a 3 year energy goal, a 1 year roadmap and 90 day priorities. Once we have those three areas in place we are able to create weekly action steps to stick to and be held accountable.

The 3 year goal is more of a vision. It includes why you are working toward this goal, your lifestyle, and the support system you have in place to be able to make this high energy lifestyle yours.

The 1 year roadmap is what you will get in a year, with specific metrics that are undeniable.

The 90 day priorities is how to get there, including the 3 key areas you will focus on and the healthy habits you will create.

The weekly plan will be the one thing you will do this week to make sure you are going to hit your goals. This makes hitting your goals simple and you will be better poised to accomplish any goal you set your mind to.

The Way I Look At Water And How it Changed My Energy Levels Forever

When I weighed 265 pounds, I used Snapple and orange juice to get hydrated. I did not know that I was just getting a sugar high and I was actually dehydrating myself from the toxins and acids in those drinks.

I was never a coffee drinker but I heard that if you want to have great energy you have to start drinking coffee. I tried it and the taste was not for me. Coffee tastes like burnt paper to me. I know, most people love coffee, I'm a weirdo. I am ok with that.

Once I started running, something strange happened. When I got home, I was thirsty and sweaty. I didn't think it would be wise to drink orange juice as my body was craving real water.

After my workouts, I started drinking water. My body naturally reached for water instead of snapple and orange juice.

A trainer once saw me drinking a snapple and told me, "Joe, never drink your calories, it's such a waste. Water is the only thing you should be drinking if you want to be healthy."

I decided to cut out all sugary drinks and within a few weeks I lost 12 pounds by just focusing on drinking water every day.

Water did not taste good to me; It was too plain. I wanted seltzer or something with flavor at first. The problem with seltzer or carbonated water, is that it fills you up before you have enough hydration.

After a few weeks of just drinking plain water, even when I did not like the taste, I started to like plain water because I got used to it. The longer I drank water the more I liked it.

What does water have to do with energy and why is it so important?

It turns out that your body is mostly water. I mean over 80% water! That means that if you want to be healthy and have energy you need to fill your body up with water each day.

You lose water every time your breathe. Don't believe me? Go outside on a cold winter day and exhale. Do you see the moisture leaving your body? That happens all day and all night. You lose liters of moisture via your breath. You need to refuel your water resources throughout the day to make sure that you have the energy you need to feel good.

A 5% drop in hydration is a 30% drop in energy!

Most people think that they need to eat when they have low energy or when they feel hungry. It is true, we must eat, but if instead you try and drink water, you might realize that you are just thirsty. By drinking water, you will feel satisfied without eating those extra calories.

When I started drinking over 100 ounces a day, it felt like I was going to the bathroom every few minutes. The adult bladder is only 16 ounces in size. When you drink 16 ounces of water, you will need to expel much of that water within the next 2 hours.

That means that if I drink a cup of water every hour, I will need to use the bathroom every 2 hours.

So, if my stomach is 32 ounces, and my bladder is 16 ounces, how much water should I drink a day? After speaking to dozens of experts and reading many articles, I learned that I should drink half my weight in ounces. That means, if you weigh 200 pounds you should drink 100 ounces per day. There are 8oz in a cup so 100/8 = 12.5 cups per day.

Another thing I noticed is that each gulp of water that I take is about an ounce. So when I can't measure, I make sure to count the gulps. My goal is to take 8 gulps an hour.

What really fires me up in the morning is the first 16 ounces of water. Not only does it wake me up, but it wakes every aspect of my body up. I just spent an entire evening getting rid of water, time to fill up again.

Adding lemon to the water is an great way to get extra flavor and to get vitamin C into your body. Lemon also helps you alkalize, which keeps your body in a better, healthier, more energetic state.

A Doctor did over 3000 studies on how water heals most ailments. He documented his studies on his website www.watercure.com. If you want to learn more about his findings, check it out.

"You're not sick; you're thirsty. Don't treat thirst with medication." - Dr. F. Batmanghelidj

How do you do know if you are dehydrated? If you feel thirsty, it's too late; you are already dehydrated. Instead check your urine.

Monitor your urine to make sure you are not dehydrated:
- A hydrated body produces clear, colorless urine.
- A somewhat dehydrated body produces yellow urine.
- A severely dehydrated body produces orange or dark-colored urine.

If you want to make sure you drink enough water, buy a Contigo water bottle and keep it near you all the time. Take a sip a few times each hour or get a water app to remind you when it's time to drink another cup of water.

Water has changed my life and now I use it to get energized instead of other fluids which do the opposite!

There is one more benefit that water has that most people do not know about.

When you put food into your body, your body turns it into energy and if it is excess food, it will store it as potential energy.

One of the ways that the body will shed fat is via urine. A lot of people that are overweight do not drink enough water and as a result, they are not allowing their body to shed the fat. Even if they diet and restrict the calories they eat, they might not gain more weight but they remain stagnant because they have not been drinking enough water each day.

Your body cannot process more than 1 liter of water per hour, so please make sure not to drink too much water at a time, I recommend drinking 8 ounces per hour, every hour.

Your kidneys can't filter more than 27-33 ounces (0.8-1.0 liters) per hour. Therefore, in order to avoid hyponatremia symptoms, you should not drink more than a liter of water per hour, on average.

Remember to balance everything you do so you can have the right amounts of high energy. Now let's talk about foods!

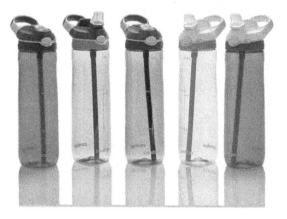

Key Takeaways About Water

- Your body is mostly water, it keep your body hydrated.
- Water gives you energy, drink it every hour.
- Drink half your weight in ounces every day to stay hydrated.
- Drink 16 ounces every two hours, you will go to the bathroom every two hours.
- Your urine should not be dark, it should be clear if you are well hydrated.
- Fat leaves your body via urine so make sure you drink enough water to lose that fat!.
- Don't overdrink water, keep the right balance.
- If you are not eating, add electrolytes to your water to stay hydrated.

5 Foods That Are Making You Fat And Keeping You Fat

What creates fat in your body? I used to think that it was the fat that was in foods. When you eat fat, you get fat. What does bread have to do with it?!

I love bread. I love crusty bread. I love jelly beans and gushers but what I did not realize was that it was making me fat.

My brother came over to me and asked me for a shortcut to lose the 100 pounds he had gained over 5 years of being married. I told him that if he wants to take a shortcut to lose weight, he will end up gaining it all it all back again. Some people call that the yo-yo diet.

My mother lived on the yo-yo diet, gaining and losing weight her whole life.

The key to success is understanding how to maintain success.

There are five foods that I realized I needed to cut out of my life while I was losing weight. These 5 foods are very common and what they all have in common is that they are not dense in nutrients, but instead create fat in your body as the energy is not used right away.

People are shocked when I give them these five simple ingredients because they are a staple of most items we eat today.

When I tell them to stop eating these 5 things for 90 days and see what happens to their fat levels, they are shocked with the results because it's true. You will lose weight when you cut out these 5 things. It worked for me, it worked for my brother and it worked for every person I ever coached through this process.

High Energy Secrets

Like I said earlier, I am not a doctor or a nutritionist, I can only share my experience here. Please consult your doctor before you do anything that I share in this book.

Since I cut out these 5 ingredients from my regular diet, I have more energy than I ever had my entire life.

Here are the 5 things you must cut out if you have lots of weight to lose.

1. Flour
2. Sugar
3. Rice
4. Potato
5. Pasta

When I tell people this they look at me funny and say, "Are you nuts? What am I going to eat when I am hungry?" I say, "Have you considered nuts?"

Seriously, if you don't want to lose weight, keep eating sugar. Keep eating french fries and breads. They are freakin' delicious. Not very nutritious, but they are addictive and taste and smell so good. They are irresistible and I did not stop eating them until I learned it's poison for me and it takes away my energy.

Keep in mind that one thing all these foods have in common is that they are not very nutrient dense. That means that for each calorie, you are getting emptiness. Your body doesn't get what it needs from these foods and it just stores them as fat if you don't use their energy right away.

I have a carb credit limit and if I want to avoid going into carb debt, I need to make sure that I don't overeat each day.

When you spend more than you make, you end up gaining debt. It's simple math, but how many people do you know that are up their neck in debt? It's not because they don't make money, it's because they spend more than they make.

Same thing with eating foods. If you eat the wrong foods and your belly keeps getting bigger, you are getting into debt and the longer you wait and the more you spend the harder it is to climb out.

I found this crazy graphic on Google that shows the time that people started to view fat at the source of people getting fat, instead of carbs. Look what happened to obesity levels.

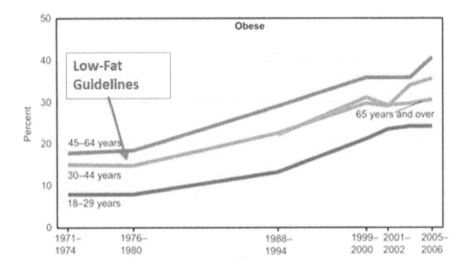

It shows how when people started intaking sugar, obesity levels started to skyrocket. People started worrying about low fat. That is not the problem!

If you want to lose weight cut it out. No sugar, no fake sugar. NOTHING! Sugar itself is not what causes fat. Carbs cause your body to store fat!

It's the body that creates the fat when sugar gets into the body. So even if you eat FAKE sugar like diet soda, the body will find other things you eat to turn those things into fat. Cut it out for 90 days and see how your body changes.

People often ask me, what about whole wheat bread and whole wheat pasta. Can I eat those things and lose weight? I say you can eat anything and lose weight over time but the fastest way to lose weight is to cut out all carbs from your diet.

Whole wheat is not really whole. It has tons of regular flour that makes your body store energy you do not need if you are not running a marathon.

What about sushi, isn't it healthy? Not if you want to lose weight. The rice makes you fat. You also won't feel full because these types of foods are missing fiber so you end up eating much more than one serving.

Are you willing to commit for 90 days not to eat these 5 things? I personally committed never to eat those 5 things if I am over my personal weight limit. As I write this book, I weigh 175 pounds, and my goal is to stay in the 170's. If I get into the 180's I cut out the 5 things and watch as my weight goes back down.

I can enjoy french fries and bread once in a while but I know if I continuously abuse those foods, I will get into debt and I need to be responsible if I want to have high energy!

Keep in mind that every time you eat carbs, you are setting the clock back two weeks till your body gets into fat burning mode. It's OK if you are not in a rush and want to lose weight over a long period of time, but if you want results sooner, you need to cut them out completely.

It takes two weeks for your body to get off the sugar and wheat addiction and convert to burning fat instead of sugar. What would you rather burn, sugar or fat? Read on to learn more!

"The food is the disease, Eliminate The Food - Eliminate the problem."

- Joe Apfelbaum

Are You Burning Sugar or Fat? Pick Your Fuel

Once I cut out those 5 foods from my diet, I had really bad cravings for at least two weeks. But, something magical happened after two weeks of not being on carbs. I stopped craving carbs completely.

I also stopped becoming hangry. That means being thrown into a rage when I don't get my sugar fix.

When I learned that your body can either burn fats or sugars, I finally understood why my body was not losing fat each day even when I was lowering my carb intake and was exercising.

You won't burn fat if your body is in the mode of using carbs as fuel. You need to starve your body of that type of fuel. It will take 2 or 3 weeks, but then your body will start getting fuel from fats. It has to do with lowering the production of the hormone insulin in your body. When your body produces lots of insulin, it stores fat instead of using the fat you have stored up. Carbs and sugars cause your body to produce fat storing insulin.

Once you starve your body of carbs, as long as you are hydrated, you will see the pounds start to fall off. Because you will begin running on fat for energy instead.

If you stuff your face with any one of the 5 carbs, your body will get back into running off of sugar and you will need to wait another two weeks of zero carbs to convert back to burning fat. Some people say you can convert to fat in a day, but I prefer to think about it as two weeks so I behave in a way that will gets me to my goal faster.

I read this amazing book: The Art and Science of Low Carbohydrate Living: An Expert Guide to Making the Life-Saving Benefits of Carbohydrate Restriction Sustainable and Enjoyable by Stephen D. Phinney and Jeff S. Volek. In it, they explain all the science behind why this works.

I was fascinated when I learned that you can choose your fuel, but you can only choose one at a time.

Which source of energy fuel is your body running on?

7 Daily Reminders That I Think About Every Day.

It takes hard work to keep up my high energy lifestyle. It's not something that I can set and forget. I need reminders every day to do the things that matter most.

I realized that I will never be able to do 100 things each day proactively, so I picked 7 things that I think about each day and I teach these 7 to people so they can have a more high-energy, healthy life.

Here are the 7 daily reminders.
1. Measure
2. Water
3. Appreciation
4. Communication
5. Learning
6. Contribution
7. Present

1. Measure - If you don't measure it, you can't improve it. When I heard a business mentor of mine say that, I realized that there are many things in my life that I am not measuring properly. One of those things is my weight.

The first thing that I do each morning is measure how much I weigh. I do this because that is a very important indicator to me as to where I am in my high energy goals.

I want to weigh 175 pounds and if I get over 180, I know I need to make some real changes so my weight doesn't get out of control.

The first question I ask people who ask me for advice about weight loss is, how much do you weigh now and how much do you want to weigh? I get ballpark answers and I tell them, we need awareness, strategy and accountability. Strategy is understanding your goal and how you will get to the goal and accountability is making sure you COUNT each day.

You need to have a daily log with your weight. Every day, you must weigh yourself and hold yourself accountable to where you are and what changes you will make that day, because of your newfound awareness.
Imagine you lived your life spending money like crazy, but never checked your bank account to see how you are doing. Guess what? I know people who live that way. It's a recipe for disaster. You need to check in daily so you can hit your goals.

This is why I put measure as number one. Measure it if you want to improve it.

2. Water - The second daily reminder I tell people on their journey to get healthier is to drink water. If you are not hydrated, you are not high energy. How much water did you drink today?

Water leaves your body with every breath you take. It happens every minute. You must keep yourself hydrated and you need a reminder.

For me walking around with a water bottle is helpful because it reminds me to take 8 sips every hour.

We do not really need a reminder to breath (Maybe some of us that are stressed out need to learn to breath.) But if we don't breathe, we die within minutes.

If we don't drink water, we become weak. Water and air are the most basic things we need to live and when we do not pay attention to our basic needs, we suffer.

3. Appreciation - If you don't like high energy foods and don't like to move, you will not be high energy and you won't be able to maintain that lifestyle. You need to enjoy your life to be able to live it every day. The only way to do that is to find things that you appreciate and enjoy to support your health.

What healthy foods do you love to eat? I love my smoothie in the morning. It tastes so good and it fills me up so well. I know that when I have a smoothie in the morning, I have tons of energy to get through the day.

You have to learn to enjoy aspects of a high energy lifestyle and think about those aspects so that you are compelled to engage in that lifestyle every day. I love to get out and run now! I used to hate it, but now I love it. I love the feeling right after I stop running and I get that runner's high. There's nothing like the endorphins that flow through my body after a run.

I think about enjoying a high energy lifestyle every day and it compels me to take action because we are naturally driven by the things we enjoy. We are propelled forward by our appreciation and gratitude.

4. Communication - If you don't talk about it, you don't think about it. Out of sight, out of mind. Make sure you are very social about your lifestyle. Tell people you know that you are on a journey and make it a conversation piece each day. This will hold you accountable to take action.

You might not want to be that person that sounds obsessed with health but guess what? If you want results you need to become obsessed with results!

I enjoy communicating about my journey on social media, I post my runs, my exercise selfies and my smoothies. People see my posts and get inspired to take action. It helps me stay on track each day and it also helps me celebrate my accomplishments as I get closer to my goal! That is one thing that most people oversee. You must celebrate success to make it last.

5. Learning - Not knowing how to be healthy is no excuse, you need to educate yourself. Your parents did not have the same access to information as you do. These days, in a few minutes a day, you can learn everything you need to know about what to eat, how to think, what to drink and how to improve your health.

Each day you need to be learning something about how to improve your energy levels so you can live a life that is full of power and freedom.

When we stop learning we start forgetting. Learning things that you already learned in the past is a great reminder to keep those areas of your life top of mind.

Each day I read a Blinkist (an app that summarizes books) about business, about health or about productivity. When I listen to a book summary I can quickly capture what the book is about and get some nuggets of wisdom that I can add to my day and share with others.

The days that go by where I do not pay attention and learn something new, are not fulfilling because learning is progress and applied learning is where you actually get results.

6. Contribution - One of the thoughts that used to go through my head all the time was: "Who am I to tell you what you should be doing. I am not a doctor or nutritionist. How dare I attempt to give people advice about their health. There are people who are more qualified than me. I should keep my mouth shut!"

I also had people tell me not to give the world advice because I might be wrong. What I realized is that the very people giving me advice about not sharing my ideas about health are often overweight and have lower energy than me. I have amazing experiences that I must share with others and the best way for me to stay motivated is to contribute to others that are interested in maintaining a high energy lifestyle.

The best feeling in the world for me is to support someone else like me on their journey. We are all going through our personal journeys and when you make the time to help someone else in theirs, it feels good and motivates you to keep going on your own journey.

How do you contribute? Buy someone this book, take them to a class with you, give them a tip that you got and follow up to see the results!

7. Present - There is no greater gift that you can give yourself than being in the moment. I know, it sounds cliche, but it's something that has given me lots of value as a daily reminder.

I get so caught up on where I want to be tomorrow and where I was yesterday, I forget about the here and now.

Put your fork down for a minute. I really mean a full minute. Savor the food in your mouth and enjoy the company that you are with. Take a deep breath and feel your surroundings.

Get out of your head and just experience life for a moment.

Practice this last one everyday so you can live a more stress free life. Stress and worry only happens when we get into our heads. A mentor once told me that if you are in your head, you are dead!

So be alive, get out of tomorrow and into today for at least a moment each day. You never know when will be the last moment you get to enjoy.

Joe Apfelbaum

7 Daily Reminders Recap:
- Measure the indicators that will help you get to your goals each day.
- Drink water to have energy and keep a bottle around you all the time so you remember to drink.
- Find healthy foods that you actually appreciate, and enjoy eating healthy foods daily.
- Communicate your goals with the people who will hold you accountable each day.
- Learn about your body, your health and how to keep getting better daily.
- Contribute to others to stay motivated daily.
- Be in the moment and enjoy the now!

These 7 reminders are the ones that keep me going and if a day goes by and I am not feeling high energy, or I am not really feeling powerful, I ask myself: Am I keeping these 7 daily reminders top of mind? Start with one a week for 7 weeks and stack them on, till you start getting the results you want in your life.

Inspiring my brother Yehuda to go for a run in Prospect park

Why Movement Is So Important and How to Get Going Everyday.

I was never the type of person who liked to go for a run or break a sweat. My body was built to sit on a couch and be on my phone or be on the computer all day. I felt most comfortable when I just relaxed and worked on the computer or on the sofa.

One day I was listening to a seminar about health and I heard a guru talk about the lymph fluid in your body. He said that the blood is known as the river of life and it has a powerful pump built into it. Your heart pumps about 2000 liters of blood each day and recirculates the 5 quarts of blood that you have in your system daily. Blood travels all over your body and distributes all the oxygen and nutrients your cells need to thrive.

The thing is, your cells need cleaning as well in order to be healthy. The blood does not clean the cells. There is another type of fluid in the body that cleans the cells - it's call the lymph fluid. This system touches every tissue in your body and it eliminates the waste from your cells. The problem is that it does not have a built in pump to move that fluid around.

There is 3 times more lymphatic fluid in your body than there is blood. To be healthy and clean, you really need to get that fluid moving each day. Clean cells are full of energy. Deep breathing is a good way to get the fluid moving but the best way is to run and jump each day.

I discovered that after I go for a run, I feel this amazing feeling of clean energy all over my body. The same feeling I get after I dance at a good, high energy wedding. It's partly because my cells are feeling cleaner than ever.

High Energy Secrets

Feeling down? Get moving! You must do this so your cells can be healthy. Walk like you are late. Do some jumping jacks. Get an inexpensive rebounder and get your fluids moving.

Once you start to feel the benefits of moving around and being active you won't look at movement as a burden anymore. It will become a treat for your body.

Exercise is a form of therapy for me to stay grounded. Every weekend I walk for at least 7 miles and during that 2 hour walk, I get cleaned out. My mind calms down and I get my best ideas.

Instead of moving being a burden to me, it becomes a benefit because I understand that it's something that I must do to clean my cells and have amazing energy.

When I was a child, brushing my teeth was a burden. Now that I understand how plaque builds up and that I want my breath to smell nice, I know that it's a benefit to me to brush my teeth. It's the same with exercise and movement.

The best way to get moving is to put on exercise gear in the morning so you are wearing the uniform of action! It helps me mentally prepare to go for a run.

What types of movements will you start to implement in your life?

Taking one of my famous jump shots at Grand Army Plaza in Brooklyn on a rainy day.

"To create the right emotions, you must first create the right motions."
- Joe Apfelbaum

What Goes Into My Green Smoothie Every Morning

When you look at your plate do you see mostly brown foods that are sweet or salty? Proteins and starches used to fill up my plate each day. Also known as meat and potatoes, meatballs and rice, steak and fries etc.

What I realized was that after I eat brown foods and lots of protein, I actually have less energy, not more energy. The digestive system is the most energy intensive system in the body and to process all the calorie dense foods, your body needs to work hard. Especially if you are mixing carbs and proteins, your body will work twice as hard.

One of the things I started to do each morning to put more nutritious food into my body is to prepare a smoothie.

We need to have lots of greens each day to stay healthy. The fastest way for me to consume 2 - 3 ounces of spinach in the morning is to drink it in a smoothie.

This power drink helps me give my digestive system a break because all the foods that I consume are broken down and liquified into a smoothie for my body.

The nutrients are very accessible and my body can focus on taking those nutrients and distributing them to the places it needs them most.

People often ask me what I add to my smoothies. Here are a few ingredients.

1. **Water**: I always add a base of at least 12 ounces of water to the smoothie. The thicker I want it to be, the less water I add, but I like it runny so I can knock it down fast.
2. **Greens**: I add around 3 ounces of spinach or kale. I usually alternate every week between spinach and kale to give my body a break from having one type of green. I make sure to freeze my greens so I can preserve them as they tend to go bad quickly if I leave them in the refrigerator for many days. Plus if they are frozen, it is easier to break them down.
3. **Psyllium Husk**: I add one tablespoon of Psyllium Husk to my smoothie. Most of us do not have enough fiber in our diet. We need fiber to help our body get rid of waste and lower cholesterol. If you don't have a regular bowel movement, this will help soften your stool and get you going like clockwork. Keep in mind that you must be hydrated in order for fiber to work.
4. **Hemp Seeds**: I make sure to add a tablespoon or two of hemp seeds to my smoothie because they're full of great nutrients. They also contains omega 3 and protein.
5. **Chia Seeds**: Adding a few tablespoons of chia seeds also adds more omega 3s and protein, but they also add healthy fiber to my smoothie. Some people say you need to soak them for them to be effective.
6. **Lemon**: I love the zest that lemon adds to my smoothie so I squeeze a whole fresh lemon into my smoothie. It's full of vitamin C and adds great flavor.
7. **Frozen Fruit**: I add some strawberries, blueberries, mangos or pineapple to my smoothie, as available. Fruit adds sweetness and some really great antioxidants and nutrients. Be careful not to add too much fruit because it's high in sugar. Use fruits that are in season as they are naturally sweeter, and watch your serving size, it's easy to get carried away.

Sometimes I also add an apple or some carrots. Other times I'll add some chopped walnuts or almonds. It all depends on how I am feeling and what is available.

Mix it up and see what you enjoy. The key is to make it enjoyable so that you feel it's a treat.

When I drink my smoothie, I also take my vitamins with it. I make sure to finish the entire smoothie within a few minutes because otherwise I get full and I can't finish it.

This 16 to 20 ounce drink fills me up for most of the day. As long as I drink water, it gives me energy for many hours and I do not feel like I need to snack.

What do you put in your smoothie?

Taking my smoothie to go while I walk my son to school.

The Secret of Apple Cider Vinegar

I am constantly testing out new ways to feel amazing energy. Besides drinking enough water and moving each day, I discovered that adding a few tablespoons of apple cider vinegar to my diet routine gives me more energy.

There are many recorded benefits to raw, unfiltered, unpasteurized "With The Mother", organic apple cider vinegar that has been recorded throughout history. The best way to feel the benefits is to try it out for yourself.

I usually have 2 tablespoons of raw organic apple cider vinegar in 12 - 16 ounces of water. I drink it at one time. Some people like to add honey or stevia to it, I just drink it plain. When I started drinking it, I did not like the smell or the taste but I got used to it over time. It kind of tastes like apple juice to me now.

Here are some of the benefits of Apple Cider Vinegar.

- Contains Acetic Acid which helps get rid of bad bacteria and fosters good bacteria in the body. It acts as a natural antibiotic and helps you heal your body.
- It cleanses your liver and helps make sure that you have a good immune function so your body is fresh to fight diseases. This is because it helps balance the body's PH balance so it's perfect for a detox.
- It can get rid of bad yeast in your body which is the source of bad breath and fungus.

There are many more benefits to apple cider vinegar but you need to try it for yourself to see the effect it has on you personally.

Mojovation Cocktail Recipe

One of the things that happen to us when we stop eating carbs and we increase our water intake, is that we start losing some of the minerals in our body called electrolytes.

In order to make sure to keep up your sodium and potassium levels, I decided to create a cocktail that keeps me energized each morning. I got inspired by watching Youtube videos and reading up on the effects of sodium and potassium on your energy levels. As with everything in this book, speak to your doctor before you try this.

Here is what I put into my amazing Mojovation Cocktail.

- 16 ounces of purified water or natural spring water. (Think Evian or SmartWater)
- ¼ teaspoon of pink himalayan sea salt which has about 500mg of sodium
- ¼ teaspoon of no-salt or salt free which has about 600 mg of potassium
- ¼ teaspoon of cayenne pepper. (Will make you feel warm, has many health benefits, improves weight loss, metabolism, detox etc.) (Very hot but you can get used to it.)
- 2 tablespoons of organic raw apple cider vinegar with the mother. (Optional)
- Half a freshly squeezed lemon (Optional and very refreshing)

If I am fasting, I drink that every 3 hours to stay hydrated - The most important part of this cocktail is the electrolytes which means the sodium and potassium.

This is only effective when you stop eating carbs because your kidneys get rid of the sodium in your body at a faster pace so you want to make sure that you have the daily recommended allowance which is about 2000mg for a healthy adult. The key is to drink enough water to flush it out. If you don't drink 2 liters or more a day you will not be able to properly flush your system out.

The more sodium you take, the more water you need to balance it. It will also make it easier for you to eliminate your waste when you have the daily recommended sodium and potassium.

Speak to a doctor before you do this to make sure that you won't have any complications.

"A 5% drop in hydration is a 30% drop in energy."
- Joe Apfelbaum

My Mother Taught Me That I Was A Night Person, Now I Am An Early Bird.

Oh no! It's 9:30 am and I am still in bed! I have a client meeting at 10:15 am at the office. I have to scramble like crazy to get to the office on time. Maybe I should let them know that I will be late.

Why am I always getting up late? I guess I am just not a morning person… I just do not have the energy to do good work in the morning. It's useless!

My mother always taught me that there two types of people. Night people and morning people. My father was a morning person, he would get up before everyone and go to sleep early. My mom, on the other hand, was a night person, she would be up as late as possible. She told me that I was like her, a night person.

I was not to blame for getting up late and not having high energy in the morning. It's just part of my DNA.

Armed with that information, I lived my life as a night person. Usually relying on my second wind. My thought process was, even if I wanted to go to sleep early, it's no use because I am a night person, I was built to do my best work at night. That rational got me sleeping in most mornings resulting in a reactive instead of proactive life.

Now, I get up at 5am and have time to write books like this one. I have an amazing morning routine that allows me to prepare myself so that I really have a productive day.

People often ask me what changed? How did I start getting up at 5 am and become so productive so early in the morning?

I once heard someone say that the most successful people wake up the earliest. As I started to meet CEOs of companies that made hundreds of millions in profit, and billions of dollars in annual sales, I decided to ask them what time they got up in the morning. To my surprise they all said they were up before 6 am, many before 5am. They went on to describe their morning routines which never entailed rushing out of bed as late as possible and shoving a Danish down their throat on the way to another late meeting.

I started to research how to get up early because I was interested in reaching those levels of success. Success leaves clues and I was searching for them. Being proactive and starting my day early became something I would constantly obsess over.

At first, I would wake up exhausted and was really not in the mood to be making such a life change. I couldn't understand how people could do it.

I read a book called "The Miracle Morning" by Hal Elrod and I realized that there are practical steps to getting up early in the morning and feeling energized. It all begins with understanding how many hours of sleep you need in order to fully recharge yourself.

When you sleep, your body has time to repair itself and to cleanse your brain. That is why it's important not to eat at least 2 to 3 hours before you go to sleep. This way you don't use all the energy digesting food while you sleep. Instead, you use the energy to repair the cells in your body.

It's important to hydrate before you sleep, so, make sure you drink a full cup of water before you go to bed.

How many hours of sleep do you think you need?

When I started researching sleep, I learned that we sleep in 90-minute cycles. Here is a quick blurb I found online.

High Energy Secrets

"The **sleep cycle**: A **sleep cycle** lasts about **90 minutes** and **during** that time we move through five stages of **sleep**. NREM **sleep**: Across these four stages we move from very light **sleep during** Stage 1 down to very deep **sleep in** Stage 4. ... This is the stage of **sleep in** which most dreaming occurs."

I need between 4 - 6 cycles of sleep to feel energized all day long. The one that is the most important is the last one. That means 6 or 7.5 hours is best for me personally.

The only way to know how much sleep you need is to test it out yourself and see how you feel during the day. The most important part is to keep a sleep log to create an awareness of how many hours you are getting each night.

Most people don't know about the cycles of sleep and are not aware of how much time they spend sleeping. I know. I was in that boat and I would just make excuses about being a night person and not a morning person.

Once you are logging your sleep, you will see patterns. The later you go to sleep, the less energy you will have when you wake up.

Set a bedtime and a wake up time. For me, when I need to be super productive, my bedtime is 10pm and my wake up time is 4am. That gives me 6 hours of sleep. When I want to take it easy and rest, my bedtime is 10pm and my wake up time is 530am.

If I want to make sure I am asleep by 10pm, I must first turn off my electronics by 9 and start getting into bed because I know that I will have interruptions due to my 5 young children.

When I started doing this consistently, I realized that my energy levels in the morning were higher than at night, and, I was being more creative in the morning.

Now that you understand what it takes to properly rest and to be able to get up earlier in order to have higher energy, you can get started.

Create a sleep log and track what time you go to sleep each day and what time you wake up. Also include how well you slept that night. A Fitbit that you wear as a watch will measure how well you sleep.

Decide how many hours you need each night based on how you feel during the day after 6 hours of sleep or 7.5 hours of sleep and set a bedtime and a wake-up time in accordance with your findings.

Once you have those two things set up, you can decide if you are a morning person or a night person.

Let's review a killer morning routine next.

The Amazing Morning Routine That Doubles My Energy

"The world belongs to the energetic."
--RALPH WALDO EMERSON

When I started getting up early, I didn't really have much energy and I wondered what it would take to get more energy in the morning. How do you ramp up your energy levels to be able to skip and jump and get everything done with level ten energy?

There were a few hacks that I needed to learn to help me to properly wake up.

Once I learned what worked for me, I created a morning routine that I easily follow.

Here is a morning routine that does not give me energy.

1. Wake up as late as possible and fight with the alarm clock.
2. Check my phone while in bed and stay in bed as long as possible.
3. Drag myself out of bed and wash my hands.
4. Quickly take a shower and get dressed because I am late.
5. On the way to my late meeting grab an orange juice and a Danish.
6. Feel bad because I never see my kids off to school.
7. Wonder if I missed something because my emails keep piling up.
8. Realize that now I will need to work till 3am again to get caught up.

Here is a morning routine that supports higher energy levels.

1. Wake up at 530 am and realize that I had 7.5 hours of sleep.
2. Weigh myself and do my power move because I am down 90 pounds.
3. Wash my hands and put on my running gear.
4. Drink 16 ounces of water to rehydrate myself in a fully lit room. Add apple cider vinegar and take my vitamins to really wake me up.
5. Have plenty of me time to write a book, journal, meditate, exercise, pray and share my ideas on social media.
6. Make a smoothie with amazing ingredients that will fill me up and keep me going.
7. Clear out my inbox and list out the three most important things I need to do.
8. Send my kids off to school and get to my first meeting early.

The key is to keep things simple. People ask me what the most important thing for an amazing morning routine is, and I always say to keep it simple. Start small, if you want to lose weight, start by weighing yourself each morning and drinking 16 ounces of water. Don't add too many things because you will end up giving them all up.

Bad habits are replaced one at a time with good habits. If you have a habit of drinking coffee first thing in the morning, replace that habit with drinking water first thing in the morning. Do that for 30 days and see how you feel. If you have a habit of eating a Danish, replace that habit with a fruit smoothie each morning. It might have the same amount of calories, but you will be full of powerful nutrients and won't have your energy levels depleted 30 minutes after you finish.

Write your routine down so you can review it each day and you do not have to think about it.

High Energy Secrets

The last thing you want to do is think about your routine. You just need to follow a checklist till it happens on its own, think building habits.

I wanted to start making my bed every morning, I added it to my list, followed the list and now it happens on its own. I do not need to have it on my list anymore. It just happens.

Think about the ideal morning routine you want to have and write it down, then start with one item at a time.

Jumping over the sunrise in Brooklyn

How I Used to Smoke a Pack a Day and Stopped Smoking Forever

Where is my lighter? My cigarette butt is getting soggy in my mouth while I look for it. Fishing in my pocket, there it is!

I covered my face with my palms so the wind does not put out the flame and I take a slow and steady pull to light myself up. Sometimes I would make O's with my lips and watch the rings float away and get larger.

When people asked me why I smoked, I would say "I just enjoy it. I am not addicted to smoking or anything, I can stop anytime I want." It was true for me, because when I decided to stop smoking, it happened in an instant.

For some people it might be much harder to stop and you might need a coach, therapy, or a patch to help.

I quit many times but I always came back to my habit when things got stressful in my business or in my relationships. Socially, I would enjoy smoking with people as a fun activity. After a big meal would be a great time for me to light one up.

The times where I would smoke the most was when I would drink. The more I would drink, the more I would want to smoke. I thought that it was the smoke entering my body and filling me up that gave me that sense of peace and stress free relaxation. No matter what was happening around me, if I was smoking, I could handle it.

Nothing anyone would say about the risks of smoking would deter me. People would say, "You know that smoking causes cancer?" I would reply that I know many old people that lived long wonderful lives and smoked most of their lives.

High Energy Secrets

I knew deep down that I was wrong, that it was bad to smoke, and it was terrible for my breath too. When I stopped smoking, I hated the smell of smoking on other people when they came in from a cigarette break. It would make me nauseous and give me headaches.

What changed my attitude toward smoking forever was when I came to the realization that smoking is really just deep breathing!

I learned that when we are stressed, we are just not breathing.

Think about it. You are in a traffic jam and there is no way out. You now realize that you will be late to one of the most important meetings of your life. You start to worry and get majorly stressed out. What will you do? How will you get out of this mess? What will happen to your family or your business if you miss this meeting because of the stupid traffic? You should've left earlier! The guilt starts and you start beating yourself up.

Suddenly, it's a miracle, the traffic opens up and there is no one in front of you. You realize you will be 30 minutes early! You will have plenty of time to prepare and be able to ace this meeting.

What is the first thing you do when you realize you are in the clear? You take a deep breath and sigh of relief as you exhale.

That is exactly how we smoke! We take deep breaths in and let it out slowly.

Joe, do you mean to say that I can breathe deeply and have the same effects on my relaxation as smoking without the bad breath, smelly clothing and harmful long term health risks?

Yes! Breathing is what makes us calm, not smoking.

Try to smoke without breathing, not fun at all!

Once I realized that, I started deep breathing when I feel stressed or anxious and the feeling really goes away.

Running actually forces me to breathe deeply and instead of just smoking for 5 minutes, I can run for 30! I get more energy than smoking a pack a day and it's FREE.

It's a no brainer now because I finally understand my body and how I can have more energy.

Now, I have these conversations with smokers and some get it, but they prefer to keep smoking because it's a social thing.

They say that you are the average of the 5 people you spend the most time with. I stopped spending time with people who smoke. I realized something incredible. When I spend time with people that are obsessed with health and high energy, I become more obsessed and, in turn, healthier.

I also noticed by meeting a few thousand successful CEO's, that 99% of them do not smoke. Most of them tried it, but quit once they found other ways to relax and maintain their energy levels.

Now that you know how important breathing is, take a deep breath and enjoy it guilt-free.

Stress saps our energy away and the only thing that will calm you down is by breathing deeply.

That is what meditation is all about. People think that it's about controlling your mind.

No! Meditation is becoming aware of your breath, your body, and your mind and allowing yourself to enter a state of peace and love.

High Energy Secrets

Take some quiet time away from all the noise and listen to your breath. Become aware of it and take a deep belly breath in, like you are dragging smoke down to your belly. Now let it out slowly and do this for 3 minutes with your eyes closed.

Doing this everyday has changed my energy levels forever.

How to Break Through the Plateaus and Get Unstuck.

During my journey, I have had many moments when I thought I hit my bottom. When I originally went from 265 pounds to 237 pounds, I stalled and thought I was not able to get passed that mark initially.

I thought about giving up and just accepting the fact that I was 237. I said, just enjoy life already, I lost 37 pounds!

Something inside me said, you can lose more, do not stop here. You can do it!

I found that the more I changed things up over time, the more my body responded.

When I reached a certain body weight and kept it there for at least 6 months, my body recognized that as my new body weight. It tried to keep me in that range, and, unless I massively overate and stopped working out, I would not gain much weight. But I would also not lose more weight.

I found that at each stage of my weight loss, I kept getting stuck and I would say, I will never break the 200 mark, I will never break 190, I will never break 180... But I broke them all and now, as I write this book, I am 177.7.

What needs to happen to break through the plateaus?

First you have to understand why plateaus are so frustrating!

We as humans want to feel happy and one of the things that make us happy is this thing called Progress. Yes, progress = happiness.

Progress impacts us in all areas of our life and when we understand how to create momentum which leads to progress, we can start hitting our goals faster.

When we work hard to try and hit a goal and we do not see any progress, we feel stuck, frustrated and unhappy. What do you do when you feel frustrated? I used to eat like mad and that got me to gain back the weight I had lost!

That is why people are on this thing called Yo-Yo diets. They do not understand how their bodies and minds work.

The first question I ask people who tell me they hit a plateau in their fitness and health is, "Are you really doing the three basics of nutrition; eating, exercising, and sleeping well?"

"Are you eating the right foods and not cheating at all, are you exercising and pushing yourself every day, and are you sleeping enough hours to get the full rest you need?"

If you are not doing those three things well, you need to stop wondering why you hit a plateau and realize that you really hit a self-made brick wall. You just need to get more committed and more serious and sometimes that means hiring a coach to keep you strict and accountable.

If you are doing everything right and you still are not seeing more progress, you need to check what you can change up.

Can you add more weight to your workouts? Can you do more intensity? Can you change the type of exercise you do each day?

Here are a few things I did at each stage.

1. 265 pounds. I started exercising, mostly walking, and I also I cut out sugar from my drinks and started drinking more

water. I did that for about 6 months and lost 37 pounds, I kept doing that for another 6 months and then changed it up some more.

2. 237 pounds. I cut out bread, sugar, rice, potato and pasta from my diet. I read that carbs cause fat to be created and I did not want more fat being created. Once I focused on meats, proteins, veggies etc I got down to 220 within 6 months. I kept doing that for a year and finding ways to enjoy those foods once a week on Shabbos. Kept drinking water and moving every day.

3. 220 pounds. I wanted to get down to 200 but I really was struggling. I realized that I was eating way too much milk and cheese so I cut that out of my diet after I learned how processed they are and within 6 months I got down to 200 pounds. It was the milk products and the cheeses that were not letting me lose the weight. I kept at it for another 6 months and I was down to 200 and stayed there.

4. 200 pounds. I had not seen below 200 since I was a teen! How could I do this?! I realized that I was eating tons of fruits that have sugar. I decided to cut out fruits and only eat veggies and proteins. I enjoyed eggs for breakfast with salad, fish for lunch with salad and steak or chicken for dinner with beans and salad. I also hired a trainer to teach me how to properly do pushups and squats. We did about 20 sessions together and I started to see results. On Saturday, I would enjoy anything I wanted and I still lost another 10 pounds over the course of 6 months.

5. At 190 pounds, I was stuck. I would never see the 180s. Everyone is telling me it's impossible because of my body's make-up. I already cut out everything from my diet, what else will I cut out? I started to introduce fiber into my body and I broke the 190 mark. I realized that my system needed a cleansing. I began to drink apple cider vinegar and I also started rollerblading and biking more often. I mixed it up with a T25 video workout and running and I went down to 184 in 2016.

6. 184 pounds. My body got used to being in the 180's until I went to a hotel for Passover and I said, "Let me see what happens if I eat anything I want for 7 days and do not weigh myself." I felt sick after those 7 days of carnage which turned into 2 weeks of just eating all the things that I should not have been eating if I wanted to stay in the 180s and keep losing. When I got home and weighed myself ,I was 203! I almost lost my mind. I decided to start researching the effects of animal protein on the human body and realized that if I was stuck in the 180s and I wanted to get down to 175, I needed to cut out animal protein for a short while. I cut it out for 90 days and got down to 176.5, The crazy thing was that I was feeling stronger and had higher energy than ever!

7. At 176.5 pounds, I still do not eat animal protein on a regular basis but I will eat a steak once in a while. My diet is mainly green smoothies with berries for breakfast or eggs and salad, beans and salad for lunch, and for dinner, I have veggies, salads and soups. My focus is on having lots of water and greens in my body. I add fiber to my smoothie which makes me eliminate waste each morning in a healthy way.

My goal is to never go over 175 and build more muscle but stay in the 165 - 175 range. I know what I need to do to get to that goal and now I need to stay disciplined to maintain that weight.

I eat Challah on Shabbos (Saturday) and I do not deprive myself of the occasional pizza or steak. I eat french fries when I feel like it, but most of the time, I want to eat clean because of the energy I get when I eat clean.

As long as I weigh myself every day and see where I am, I can let myself eat things that go against my goal of losing weight but still feel good about rewarding myself.

When I got to 175, I went to celebrate with a friend and ate a meal at a chinese restaurant, And I felt great after. On Thanksgiving, I ate everything I wanted to eat but I was naturally drawn to the more plant based foods, I did not get knocked out and need a nap like every other year. I was pleasantly surprised and it made me realize why I continue to eat clean.

So you still think you hit a plateau? Think again, change things up, and keep pushing towards your goal. Weight loss and health is a lifetime effort, not something you do one time and finish. Let's learn a bit about habits now.

Feeling amazing in my new suit while taking my son to school!

Enjoying All the Things You Want to Eat; Understanding Habits

Humans are creatures of habit. I know, you've heard that before. What does that really mean? That means that we use our habits as a way to survive.

We are programmed to use the least amount of energy possible to do our daily tasks so we can reserve our energy for more important, life-saving tasks.

Our bodies have a list of systems and processes that they follow and that programming was created by the circumstances in our lives.

I went to a hotel in 2015 for Passover, in Aspen, Colorado and I heard a Rabbi give a lecture about a student who had trouble learning Torah in school.

His Rabbi asked him a simple question, "Do you make your bed each morning?" The student replied that he did not make his bed and he did not understand what that had to do with being able to get up early and focus on learning Torah.

That evening the student got to his dorm room and saw his bed made perfectly with a note on his bed. The note read, "if you make your bed like this every day, you will have more success learning Torah."

The young man laughed at the notion that making your bed had anything to do with being better at learning.

Out of sheer curiosity he decided to start making his bed. He did it for a week, and it was a real chore to do each day, but it was fun to show off to his friends how he was now making his bed.

After a week he decided it was dumb and stopped doing it. His studies did not improve so he went back to the Rabbi and asked for more advice.

The Rabbi assured him that if he made his bed for 30 days he would improve his studies significantly.

The young man decided to try again, and this time, he was committed, had an accountable body, asked people for advice on how to make his bed, and he took it seriously. For once in his life, he would do a task well.

6 months passed and his learning improved dramatically. The Rabbi walked over to him and said, "Are you still making your bed?" The student honestly did not know! He ran back to the dorm room and saw that his bed was made perfectly and realized that it had become a habit.

He did not need to think about it anymore. It just 'made itself' because the machine had been programed and now, it was taking its course.

Did that make me start making my bed each morning? No! We were in a hotel in Aspen and I was not going to spend my time making my bed in a hotel.

A few weeks later, I went to a conference with CEO's, the EO Global Leadership Summit in San Diego with over 1,000 leaders from Entrepreneurs Organization from all over the world getting together to learn how to lead their chapters of 12,000 business owners that lead companies that are over 1 million in revenue.

At one of the workshops, a man named Dandapani gave a talk about overcoming bad habits and improving our productivity. He said that the number one way to improve yourself is to start making your bed in the morning.

I was at the edge of my seat when I heard this because I did not make my bed each day yet, but I was thinking about starting. I left that seminar early and went to my hotel room to make my bed. I committed to making my bed for 30 days and now it happens automatically.

This is when I learned how powerful a habit is. It just happens on its own once you set the programing.

All the things you do each day happen on their own.

The way you stress out when something happens that is out of your control is a habit. The way you react to a box of cookies is a habit. The way you drink water or coffee in the morning is a habit. It's all a habit!

Change your habits and change every aspect of your life. Your relationships are habits, your wealth is all about habits, your body is a sum of your habits.

I heard this saying that really stuck with me and I think about it often.

"Your beliefs become your thoughts,
Your thoughts become your words,
Your words become your actions,
Your actions become your habits,
Your habits become your values,
Your values become your destiny."

— Mahatma Gandhi

What habits do you want to create that will change your energy levels and your life forever?

Habits about how you think:

Habits about what words you use:

Habits about what you drink and how often:

Habits about what you eat:

Habits about the people you spend time with:

Habits about what time you go to sleep or wake up:

Habit about what you do when you go to work:

How to Share Your Journey With Those You Love Without Making Them Feel Bad

OMG! I just got on the scale this morning and I hit my goal!! I am at 175.4 and I am feeling amazing today! I just did a workout and I have never felt more energized.

Imagine sharing that with the world and people rolling their eyes. Thinking, "Keep your success to yourself, stop bragging already, we get it, you have great willpower Joe!"

That used to stop me from sharing my successes with the people closest to me. I was afraid I would get judged.

What happens when we are not proud of our success and we do not share them is that we are not able to celebrate as much and, therefore, our achievements do not have that much intensity.

If you get into the mindset of sharing your journey with the world you will inspire other people to set goals. Yes, some people will judge you for doing amazing things but you have to accept that as part of the process.

Sharing your progress with the people you care about or even with the people you don't care about, and getting a "Congratulations!" from them is a huge motivational push to keep working towards your goal.

I share my successes with strangers and we connect over them. I share my goals with people and they support me to get there faster.

Now there is something very important that we need to be careful about. We should never impose our own beliefs upon other people even if it's "good for them". Especially when you are in the zone and you are doing really well with your goals.

I remember, when I cut out carbs and I saw someone enjoying some warm french bread with hot butter, I would comment and say "The reason I cut out bread is because I found that it makes me so fat." That person enjoying the bread would put down the bread and feel judged. Especially if they are self conscious of their weight.

That is how you get people to resent you. It's important to be sensitive to other people and not give people advice that they have not asked for.

Coaching without permission is criticism.

If you want people to like you and get along with you and support you in your goals, never criticize, condemn or complain. It doesn't help. The best thing to do is compliment.

Instead of saying that I don't eat bread now, I take a piece of bread and I jokingly smell it. I talk about how addictive eating bread is and how I would eat the whole thing if I started eating one piece. I ask questions and I am naturally curious instead of coaching people that did not ask to be coached.

If I see someone with low energy, I ask, "How much water do you generally drink a day?"

They usually look at me and say "Not enough, I don't think I drank any today."

I take a sip of my water and say, "Wow, on days that I don't drink water, I really have no energy. May I share a secret about water that I learned on my journey?" Usually I get a YES.

Now I've got permission to coach! "A 5% drop in hydration is a 30% drop in energy!"

High Energy Secrets

As they take a glass of water, they will ask for more stats or ask me about going to the restroom too often and I launch into my journey because they've asked for it. Now I can be proud and share.

Be proud of your accomplishments, it's not EGO if you actually accomplished what you are sharing and it's super motivating to share with others.

What do you like to share with people about your journey?

How to Read Nutrition Facts on Things You Buy in the Store

We were sitting at a conference together, and I asked my coworker, "How many calories do you think this has?"

He looked at the bag of nuts and said "130. It says it right there on the label enlarged and in big letters."

I looked and he was right. It was written in really big letters. 130!

That does not seem like a lot of calories for this MASSIVE bag of nuts.

I started eating the nuts and realize that it was not really 130 calories. It was actually 390 calories!

How did I make that mistake?

Let's go back a few years to my childhood.

I remember slurping down spoonfuls of Post Fruity Pebbles cereal with blue milk while reading the back of the cereal box.

Why blue milk? Because I thought it was healthier than red milk. I mean, if you want to be *really* healthy, you need to drink green milk but I was not at that level yet.

This is the extent of the health knowledge that I had growing up.

I'm sure that you are different and you read labels and understand nutrition facts but I realized that there are some things that I never looked at that blew my mind away.

High Energy Secrets

Most people look at calories, but once you learn about how your body produces calories and how much energy you have after eating different foods you realize that not all calories are created equal.

Also, calories are misleading. Especially if you do not look at serving size! You eat a container of cookies that says it only has 20 calories per serving. Wow, I can really enjoy all these cookies for 20 calories?

Did you take the time to keep reading how many cookies per serving? Did you realize that when you eat the box of cookies you are essentially eating 3,000 calories?

I know that I did not make that calculation. Even when I was reading the label.

When you are in the Jar, you cannot read the label. When I am eating cookies, I am usually in that jar!

A bottle of Coke says it only has 250 calories but it has 2.5 servings! That means you are actually drinking 600 calories for each bottle you consume.

Serving size is very important and I never realized how companies mess with our perception to be able to make statements that will affect the way people consume their products.

There are 7 things I look at when I read nutrition facts these days.

The first thing I look at is how many grams of sugar the product has. I will not eat anything that has more than a few grams of sugar per serving. It will destroy my energy levels.

The second thing I look at is protein because my brain feeds off the protein in foods. I want to be aware of how much protein foods have. It's more about awareness than anything else. Not all foods need to have protein but if they have good amounts of protein like beans, I keep that in mind when I make my food choices.

The third thing I look at is ratio of fiber to carbs. You want to make sure that for every 7 grams of carbohydrates, there is at least one gram of fiber. Some people say that a 10 to 1 ration is enough, other people want to be more aggressive and say you need a 5 to 1 ration.

Realize that if the food has 30 grams of carbs and zero fiber you want to be very careful before you consume that food because it will create some issues with your energy levels.

To maintain my ratio, I use a fiber supplement in my diet with psyllium husk each day. That helps me regulate my levels. Just something to keep in mind when browsing those nutrition facts.

The fourth thing I look at is the ingredients. If the first ingredient is sugar and the second is corn syrup, the third might as well be poison!

Ingredients often have chemicals that are very dangerous in high doses but your body can process them. I try to make better choices and buy foods with less chemicals like Artificial Sweeteners (acesulfame potassium, sucralose and saccharin), Synthetic Trans Fats (found in crackers, cookies, fried foods), Artificial Flavors (natural flavors are not really natural!), Monosodium Glutamate (MSG), Artificial Colors (red 40, blue 4 and yellow), High-Fructose Corn Syrup (HFCS), Preservatives (sodium benzoate, some say cause hyperactivity in kids, Sodium nitrite also causes many diseases.)

Once you start eliminating foods like these, you will start to feel much more energetic. I have a hard time in the grocery store because most food products are full of processed ingredients.

High Energy Secrets

A friend, Pamela Gold who was helping me review this book, gave me a rule of thumb: The shorter the shelf life, the longer your life.

The fifth thing I look at is serving size because it adds context to everything else I am reading on the labels.

The sixth thing I read is how many servings per container and I check the container size because this really messes with me sometimes and I have to do some math here to make sure I really get what's in this package.

The seventh thing is calories. Yes, I look at that last, because not all calories are created equal. If something has healthy ingredients and is calorie rich, I would still eat it and probably not gain weight because i'm not destroying my metabolism with garbage.

Some people ask me about fat. I don't really look at fat because most of the time, it's the sugar and chemicals that harm you, not the fat. Most people these days look at calories and fat and move on.

I found this on a website that describes it well:

For many decades, people have believed that eating saturated fat can increase the risk of heart disease.

In fact, this idea has been the cornerstone of mainstream nutrition recommendations.
However, studies published in the past few decades prove that saturated fat is completely harmless.

A massive study published in 2010 looked at data from a total of 21 studies that included 347,747 individuals. They found absolutely no association between saturated fat consumption and the risk of heart disease.

Multiple other studies confirm these findings... saturated fat really has nothing to do with heart disease. The "war" on fat was based on an unproven theory that somehow became common knowledge.

The truth is that saturated fat raises HDL (the "good") cholesterol. It also changes the LDL cholesterol from small, dense LDL (very, very bad) to Large LDL, which is benign.

There is literally no reason to fear butter, meat or coconut oil... these foods are perfectly healthy!"

Healthline.com

Now that you understand how to read nutrition facts, it's time to make it a habit to read them every time you pick up a product in the store. Shopping might take longer, but you will have more time to shop because you will live longer.

What did you learn about nutrition facts?

What Intermittent Fasting Does To Your Body

In the past, the only time I would fast was on the half dozen Jewish fast days each year and it was not a good experience.

Fasting to me was low energy, headaches, feeling like I just want to lay in bed and watch movies all day.

I did not realize that the reason I had no energy is because of lack of hydration. Once I learned that, I started researching how the effects of fasting actually help your body. What I found was that if you fast for 20 hours and just drink water you are able to get rid of fat lingering on your body at a much faster rate.

What your body does is feed off of its fat to create energy. During that time it takes all the energy that it would use to digest food and it puts your body to work at repairing your cells.

There are amazing growth hormones that the body releases while you fast for 16 hours or more that improves testosterone levels for both men and women and creates more power in your system. It helps you get rid of the toxins that your body can't get rid of while it's busy digesting food all day.

Napoleon is famous for saying something like "More people die from eating too much than from eating too little".

Once you eliminate flour and sugar from your diet you are able to fast for long periods of time while hydrated without losing energy.

For me, fasting became a game changer because I do not need to worry about eating while I am fasting. I have enough fat in my body to last me a few days of fasting and I used to have enough fat to last me a few weeks!

Fasting for 16 to 20 hours a day once or twice a week is a healthy way to detoxify.

There are certain ingredients you need to keep in your body to be able to fast and not feel low energy. Mainly, this means managing how much sodium and potassium you have in your body.

The maximum daily recommended amount of sodium has to do with how much water you drink. The more water you drink, the more the body gets rid of salt, so you need to fill yourself up with salt each day not to feel low energy.

One quick way to get your body to eliminate waste is to have a liter of water and two teaspoons of salt. Within one hour you will feel the urge to eliminate. I limit my salt to just one teaspoon per liter. You can use less if your body is already eliminating. Usually you get about 2000mg of sodium per teaspoon of salt. I like to use pink Himalayan salt because it's the most natural salt. Pink Himalayan sea salt contains over 84 minerals and trace elements including calcium, magnesium, potassium, copper and iron.

If you have too much salt, your body sheds its potassium when you urinate, so you need to balance all that sodium with the right amounts of potassium. In general, adults should get at least 4,700 mg of potassium daily, while limiting themselves to 2000 mg of sodium. But most people are not meeting either goal.

Having a teaspoon of No Salt or Salt Free (which are salt alternatives) is a great way to get in your daily allowance of potassium. You can buy that at the salt aisle in most supermarkets. Look at the nutrition facts and see how much potassium that has per teaspoon. If you have too much potassium, you will get constipated. You need to balance out the right amount of sodium and potassium in your body.

When your body is full of those electrolytes, you feel alive.

"An electrolyte is a substance that produces an electrically conducting solution when dissolved in water. ... In our bodies, electrolytes include sodium (Na^+), potassium (K^+), calcium (Ca^{2+}), bicarbonate (HCO_3^-), magnesium (Mg^{2+}), chloride (Cl^-), and hydrogen phosphate (HPO_4^{2-})."

When you have the right amounts of electrolytes in your body you realize that you do not really need to eat and you can fast for many days if you have extra fat in your body.

How do you feel when you fast? Are you well hydrated?

Milk, It Does Not Do A Body Good

I remember growing up and thinking about how milk was so good for us. People would eat milk and cookies before they went to sleep.

I used to watch commercials with the milk mustache and see how celebrities would endorse milk.

I remember on the days that I would drink lots of milk and eat milk products, I would feel sluggish and more lethargic. I did not realize that milk actually does more harm than good to my body.

I recently read this on a blog that was created to help people understand how milk is not actually good for your bones.

"The milk myth has spread around the world based on the flawed belief that this protein and calcium-rich drink is essential to support good overall health and bone health in particular at any age. It is easy to understand that the confusion about milk's imaginary benefits stems from the fact that it contains calcium – around 300 mg per cup."

But many scientific studies have shown an assortment of detrimental health effects directly linked to milk consumption. And the most surprising link is that not only do we barely absorb the calcium in cow's milk (especially if pasteurized), but to make matters worse, it actually increases calcium loss from the bones. What an irony that is!

Here's how it happens: like all animal protein, milk acidifies the body's pH which in turn triggers a biological correction. You see, calcium is an excellent acid neutralizer and the biggest storage of calcium in the body is – you guessed it... in the bones.

So the very same calcium that our bones need to stay strong is utilized to neutralize the acidifying effect of milk.

Once calcium is pulled out of the bones, it leaves the body via the urine, so that the surprising net result after this is an actual calcium deficit. Knowing this, you'll understand why statistics show that countries with the lowest consumption of dairy products also have the lowest fracture incidence in their population. (Saveourbones.com)

I do not know if this is true or not true, all I know is how I feel when I consume milk and dairy products. I feel lower energy and overall weaker when I consume milk. Try eliminating milk from your body and see how you feel, you might realize that all this cereal and milk that you have been fed is actually zapping your energy.

Instead of having milk in the morning, how about drinking water?

Enjoying smoothies with the kids for breakfast.

Eating Before You Go to Sleep; It's A Bad Idea

The best time to eat is when you wake up. Most people I know do not have time to eat a healthy breakfast because they are in a rush in the morning.

They wake up too late because they went to sleep too late and now they need to rely on coffee to keep them going.

Does that sound familiar?

I remember waking up late and going to the bakery on the way to the office to get a bottle of orange juice and an apple strudel. How I loved the sugar high I would get after knocking down that bottle! I felt so good in that moment but I crashed an hour later so I would keep snacking until I got home at night. When I got home, I would eat a massive meal and go to sleep.

This was the perfect recipe for gaining 100 pounds.

When you sleep, your body can either digest food or do necessary work on repairing itself.

If my body is going to be burning fat while I sleep, why would I want to give it a massive meal to process?

Sure, you might want to eat a healthy snack or drink some water, especially if you have the munchies. Some people say it's even healthy to do that before you go to sleep to keep up your metabolism.

I just know that my sleep is better when I eat a light meal for dinner. I try to stick to the rule of not eating at least two hours before I go to sleep.

On Friday nights, that never happens for me. I eat a massive meal and I go right to bed but it helps if I focus on veggies instead of eating lots of heavy foods.

Also, I usually get more sleep on Friday night so the extra cycle or two will help my body get what it needs.

During the week when I eat a large meal before I go to sleep, I find myself less rested when I wake up.

Do your research and see how you personally feel. Everything that experts say needs to be verified by your own personal experience.

Also, mixing heavy proteins and carbs, like meats and potatoes, before you go sleep will cause some complications in your digestion in general.

Test out not eating at least two hours before you sleep and focus on a light meal instead of a heavy dinner and see how your energy levels improve.

"The last thing you think about before you go to sleep is the first thing you think about when you wake up. Choose your thoughts wisely."
- Joe Apfelbaum

High Energy Snacks That I Enjoy Eating Guilt Free

People often ask me, "If you don't eat sugar, flour, potatoes, etc. what do you snack on?"

Here are ten things that I like to snack on that don't make me feel like I am getting fat by overeating these food products.

1. **Almonds** - When I need a quick snack, I will grab a handful of raw natural almonds and munch on them. I really enjoy them because they are so filling and satisfying. Almonds are very healthy because almonds contain lots of healthy fats, fiber, protein, magnesium and vitamin E. The health benefits of almonds include lower blood sugar levels, reduced blood pressure and lower cholesterol levels. They can also reduce hunger and promote weight loss. Watch your serving size, because binging on nuts can also cause problems.

2. **Cucumbers** - What I love about cucumbers is that they're mostly water and they keep you hydrated. Some people add cucumbers to their water but I can eat them like they are chips. Cutting up a large plate of cucumbers and munching on them is actually a treat because they are nourishing and they help you detox by flushing out toxins. Cucumbers supply skin friendly minerals and have Protein, Fiber, vitamin C, vitamin K and magnesium.

3. **Carrots & Hummus** - One of my favorite things is dipping one food into another food. I love dipping carrots into Hummus. I used to hate eating carrots. When I read about the benefits of carrots, like how they are high in Beta Carotene and how they have amazing antioxidants, I started eating them and I really enjoy them now. These root vegetables are rich in vitamin A, C, K, and B8, as well as pantothenic acid, folate, potassium, iron, copper, and

manganese. Hummus has many of those vitamins as well but it also has vitamin B. It's a great low-calorie snack that I enjoy.

4. **Frozen Blueberries** - Most people do not know this, but blueberries can actually be anti-ageing! When I heard this, I started eating more of them as a snack and in my salads. The problem with blueberries is that they go bad quickly in my fridge and it's important to eat organic ones. I realized that I can freeze them and enjoy them even more. Blueberries boost the brain, fight cancer and are just a super food in general. I snack on them whenever I can.

5. **Avocado** - Avocado is a fruit with a creamy texture. I really appreciate avocado, especially when I mash them and make them into a dip for carrots and cucumbers. I like adding lemon, garlic and sea salt to my dip. I also like cutting them into chunks and enjoying them as a snack. They're very filling because they provide a substantial amount of healthy monounsaturated fatty acids. They also have over 20 vitamins making it very nutrient dense.

6. **Edamame** - What I love about edamame is that it has protein, fiber and lots of minerals that make you feel good. I like ordering these when I go to a restaurant that offers them on the menu. I enjoy eating them warm. Sometimes I prepare frozen ones on the top of the rice cooker and enjoy them as a snack.

7. **An Apple** - An apple a day keeps the doctor away. Just keep it to one! It does contain sugar, but when you eat it in the natural state, the fiber does not let your insulin spike as much as, say, apple juice. Apples contain antioxidants, fiber and nutrients that support a healthy lifestyle and for me, it's a real treat to eat a Granny Smith apple that is super sour and delicious!

8. **Kale Chips** - Adding some olive oil to kale with sea salt and putting it in the oven will create a great healthy snack that is great for your eyes and perfect for high energy. I wondered if baking kale takes away the nutrients. I found out that baking it actually keeps most of the benefits of kale but takes away some Goitrogens which is actually great news for people who have thyroid problems that want to enjoy these leafy veggies. Do not overdo the oils, because oils are calorie dense.

9. **Dark Chocolate** - I love to eat chocolate and I always thought that it was bad for you. What I learned is that not all chocolate is created equal. You can buy chocolate that is made from cacao beans and not the processed, highly sweetened chocolate that most people eat. If you get healthy dark chocolate with a high cocoa content, you will see that it is a healthy source of nutrients.

10. **Mixed Nuts** - When I want to enjoy a healthy filling snack and mix it up a bit, I choose mixed nuts because they are high in fiber, protein and are filling. Each nut has its own health benefits and as long as they do not include random oils and sugar, you can enjoy snacking on them and get all the benefits.

Make a list of snacks that you enjoy between meals or when you are on the road so that you mentally know that you have a great variety of items you can enjoy. This way you will stay away from the gummy bears and potato chips.

When people tell me that they feel like there are no healthy options, I ramble off this list of ten options and they are shocked to see that there are more options than they think and that they are very accessible, you just need awareness and a good strategy.

What snacks do you enjoy?

"Be Proactive With Your Food and You Won't Have To Have Self Control" - Joe Apfelbaum

The Vitamins I Started Taking Daily

Some people tell me that vitamins are a scam but when I go to the Doctor and get a blood test done, they tell me that my vitamin D levels are low. I need to take a supplement or get more sun.

When I make sure to take the core vitamins I need every day to be healthy, I feel more energized and on point.

Here are some of the vitamins that I take each day.

D3 - 5000 UI of vitamin D3 - The reason I take this little gel cap each day is because vitamin D is something most people are deficient in and I know how important it is for your body. In order to be able to absorb calcium, your body needs vitamin D. If you want strong bones and to feel happier, vitamin D is known to help you feel better. It works for me.

B12 - Being that I cut back on eating meat dramatically, I was told that I need to take a supplement to make up for vitamin B that is found in meat products. B12 is not found in foods and you need this supplement to support healthy nerves and blood cells. It also helps make DNA which you need to be healthy. Read all about it here: https://ods.od.nih.gov/factsheets/VitaminB12-Consumer/

Magnesium - I realized that on days that I take my calcium with a magnesium supplement, I feel more focused. I heard that people with ADD can benefit from taking this important supplement to calm down. It also helps your body absorb calcium so I take a supplement that has both calcium and magnesium in one pill.

Vitamin C - We all have heard the importance of vitamin C and how it helps fight viruses, repair tissues and make you feel healthier than ever. I make sure that I take Ester C and not regular vitamin C because it's more PH neutral which is a different composition than regular vitamin C which has acid in it.

Psyllium Husk - Getting fiber in your body is one of the best things you can do to make sure that you feel great because you will be getting rid of the extra weight you carry around in your large intestine.

There are other things that I take from time to time like Cayenne pepper, Turmeric, Garlic extract, and Kelp which I take to feel good but not on a regular basis.

The key is to try different supplements and see if you feel better in general. Go to your Doctor and see if your blood work comes out better by taking some supplements. My Doctor was very impressed with my results.

Keep in mind that you must be well hydrated for your body to be able to benefit from any of these supplements.

When I take supplements and I do not drink enough fluids, I still feel really unstable.

The best way to remember to take supplements is to have a pill case that you fill up every week. This way, you don't have to open all the jars!

What supplements will you be taking everyday?

Becoming More Present Day To Day

There are three things that I tell every person whom I coach that they need to be able to improve in any area of their life.

Awareness, Strategy and Accountability.

Let's talk about awareness for a moment. What does it mean to have awareness?

Being 50 to 100 pounds overweight and stuffing an entire pie of pizza in your face is a lack of awareness.

Eating an entire family size bag of Wise onion garlic potato chips and knocking them down with a 32 ounce freezing bottle of Snapple is a lack of awareness.

When I used to do those things, I was not aware that I was causing my body to create havoc.

They say, you know what you know. You might even know about all the things you do not know. But you do not know what you don't know you don't know.

ALL POSSIBLE KNOWLEDGE

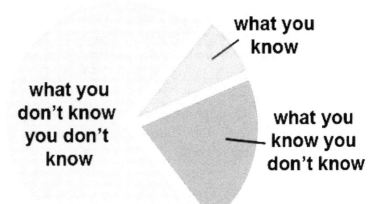

I needed to think about that statement a few times before I finally got it.

When you are wearing pink glasses, everything looks pink. Put on blue glasses and everything looks blue.

What does that have to do with having high energy? Well you might not even be present to the fact that you are losing energy by doing things, saying things and thinking things that make you lose energy.

Being present and having awareness is the first step to helping you create a strategy to improve your levels of energy and the quality of your life.

Let's begin by becoming present to our breath. Are you breathing right now? Are you aware of whether you are breathing into your chest or into your lower abdomen?

Most people are barely breathing because they are not present with the fact that they breathe only with the top of their lungs, which causes shallow breathing. That lack of oxygen does not let your brain make good decisions.

Are you sitting up straight in your chair? Do you feel your feet on the ground? How is your forehead, is it relaxed or scrunched up? What about your shoulders - do you feel like you can let go and relax? Take a deep breath and get present with your body.

When you are drinking water, do you let it swish in your mouth a bit, or do you knock it down? Are you really tasting your food or are you just inhaling everything in sight?

Look at the people around you. Really look at them and see what you notice. Are they happy? Are they being themselves? Are they stressed? Do they feel appreciated?

Look at yourself in the mirror, what do you think of how your body looks? Do you love your smile? Do you think you have eyes that sparkle? What do you love about yourself? Get more present and think about your opinion of yourself.

What questions do you have about life? If you have a meaningful conversation with God, what would you ask? What questions would be the ones you would want answers to? Write them down and think about why you would ask those questions.

When you are eating, put your fork down for a moment and look around at your surroundings.

When you go for a walk, take in the trees, the benches, the buildings or whatever you see and really be present to what you experience without judgement.

This exercise was a game changer for me because I am so bottom line driven, I was living my life without living life. If you want to experience explosive energy and really feel vitality, you need to learn to feel your life.

High Energy Secrets

To be able to feel the live energy inside you, you must become more present each day by practicing being more present.

What do you want to become more present with?

The Number One Energy Depleter, Kill Stress In 10 Seconds

Guess what the number one killer in the world is? Some would say hunger, others would say smoking or car accidents. In reality, it's stress that kills more people than anything else. Especially chronic stress that leads to all types of other complications.

When we are stressed out, we feel low energy. When we are stressed out, we are not able to think properly and come up with solutions to solve our problems. When we are stressed, our judgement is clouded by our emotions and we act in ways that we later regret.

People drink alcohol and take drugs to try and relieve stress, but, while that works short term, it's not a sustainable solution to support a high energy lifestyle.

I started studying the difference between good stress and bad stress. Why do we need stress at all and how we can avoid the bad stress in our lives?

I saw a video with Rabbi Twersky that talks about stress. He explains that we can learn a lesson about stress from a lobster. As a lobster grows inside its shell, he becomes very uncomfortable because the shell does not grow. Only the lobster grows.

At some point he is forced to go hide under a rock and leave his shell and wait for a new shell to cover his ever-growing body. He needs to keep doing this as he keeps growing.

In life, we have things that happen which make us uncomfortable. We can fight those circumstances and try not to deal with them, but the pressure will build up. Only when we learn from the events in our lives to make us grow out of our current shell, can we use the stress we feel to grow.

I heard Tony Robbins say that if you follow your stress, it will lead to your greatest fear. Fear grips us and make us stop everything.

We stop breathing too!

When we stop breathing, we stop getting oxygen.

No oxygen, no life.

No wonder stress is killing us, it's stopping us from getting oxygen to our cells.

Yes, when you fill your body with oxygen, no matter what is happening around you, you can combat stress with deep breathing and avoid the physical symptoms of stress.

Sounds simple? It is very simple but it's super hard to remember to do it when things get really bad.

Navy Seals have a training on breathing because it's easy to stop breathing when you are under fire from the enemy. You stop breathing, you stop thinking and, if you make a stupid mistake, it can cost you and your teammates their lives. They call the secret technique, Box Breathing. Here is how it works.

- Expel all of the air from your lungs.
- Keep them empty for four seconds.
- Inhale through your nose for four seconds.
- Hold for a four count (don't clamp down or create pressure; be easy)
- Exhale for a four count.
- Repeat for 10-20 minutes.

This will increase your focus, your energy and you will get rid of any physical stress that you might be feeling. It starts in 10 seconds and it will last you for hours.

People are simply not aware that they are stressed out. They are not aware that they are not breathing. Once you become aware, you need the right strategy to learn how to breathe deeply into your belly.

You also need someone who cares about you to remind you to breathe. I give my partners, friends and loved ones permission to ask me to breathe when they see I am getting stressed out about something.

There are more long-term ways to avoid getting stressed out to begin with but that takes getting deeper into the way your mind is wired to create stories about why things happen. We won't get into that right here, but keep in mind you have lots of power to increase your energy or eliminate all your energy by the repeated thoughts that you have each day.

Now that you learned how to eliminate stress from your life, let's go shopping and buy some fun things for your home and office.

"Stress means you are just not breathing. Take a deep breath and watch the stress fade away."

- Joe Apfelbaum

25 Things To Keep At Home To Promote Higher Energy

It's important to keep things that will help you stay high energy around you. Here are some things that you can keep around the house that will help you have more energy when you engage with those things.

1. **Jump Rope** - Jumping up and down will get your heart rate up really quickly and will also move your lymph nodes around so your body can do a better job at eliminating waste from your cells.
2. **Trampoline** - I make sure to keep a little trampoline in the office and in my home, also known as a rebounder, that helps me get energized before I do a call or run a webinar.
3. **Yoga Mat** - For some reason, when I have a yoga mat around I end up stretching more often. It's like putting on my running gear. I have one everywhere I go.
4. **Back Roller** - There is nothing better than having your back rolled out with a amazing back roller. This helps you relax and keeps you from getting back injuries.
5. **Resistance Band** - The easiest way to build muscle is with resistance, but you might not have room for weights in your home. Instead, just get a band that lets you build up muscle.
6. **Timer** - A great way to get motivated to stretch and do basic exercises is to time yourself. I like to keep timers around so I can do a two minute stretch or 5 minute workout.
7. **Pill Case** - When you're taking the vitamins and minerals you need, it's much easier to just get a pill case and fill up the case a week in advance so you do not have to think about it every day. You open it and go!
8. **Apple Cider Vinegar** - Raw organic apple cider vinegar is magic. Make sure it contains The Mother and you can apply it both internally and externally. It even cleans coffee machines for better tasting coffee!

9. **Hemp Seeds** - I like sprinkling these on my salads and adding them to my smoothie because of the protein and health benefits. They are not easy to find, but when I find them, I buy a big bag to keep around the house.
10. **Scale** - If you want to improve something you must measure it. I make sure that every place I visit has a scale, even my office and where I go on vacation.
11. **Palm Brush** - It's really good to brush your hair quickly, but I like brushing my face, not just because I have a beard, but because it stimulates my skin for better blood flow. I use that palm brush all over and it wakes me up.
12. **Food Scale** - Weigh your food when you do your meal preparation and make sure you understand how much you eat. You need to have a scale that measures grams and ounces so you know what you are putting into your body.
13. **Nutribullet** - A simple, inexpensive machine that will help you grind a smoothie in one minute each morning. You don't need to get a Vitamix or something expensive. One of these magical machines will do.
14. **Lemon Squeezer** - I use the lemon squeezer to quickly squeeze my lemon each morning into my mojovation cocktail. Getting one will remind you to add lemon to salads and drinks and will make sure you get every last drop out of that lemon.
15. **Frozen Fruit** - I love stocking my freezer with frozen berries and fruits that are frozen while they are very fresh. They last a really long time and they are there when I need them for a smoothie or quick snack.
16. **Raw Almonds** - Make sure to keep raw almonds around, so when you need a quick fill on something, you choose almonds. They are very filling and healthy.
17. **Journal** - When I wanted to start to write my thoughts down, I realized that if I didn't have a proper book that I called my journal, I would not be as compelled to write my thoughts down. Get a good, expensive journal and use it daily.

18. **Loudspeakers** - The best way to get motivated to dance and move around is to have loud music. Get loud speakers that will rock your world so when you do things around the house you dance!

19. **Contigo Water Bottle** - I like Contigo water bottles, because I push the button and it lets me sip water and I am also able to measure how much I drink each day. I bought one for each one of my kids and they love filling them up each day.

20. **Glass Measuring Cup** - When I want to make sure that I know how much ingredients to put into my smoothie, I like to use a glass measuring cup that is at least 32 ounces. I find that glass is easier to clean than plastic.

21. **Himalayan Sea Salt** - This pink salt is one of the most original and most mineral rich salts. It contains many benefits that will keep you healthy. I really like that it contains over 84 minerals and trace elements, including calcium, magnesium, potassium, copper and iron.

22. **No-Salt or Salt Free** - Potassium Chloride is a salt alternative and is important if you are not getting enough potassium from beans, fruits and veggies. Make sure not to take too much of this because it can cause constipation and other problems. Ask your doctor before you take any of this.

23. **Headphones You Love** - I make sure I keep a bunch of headphones around the house that I love to use so I can go for a run with music or listen to eBooks to learn or meditate to help me relax.

24. **Epsom Salt** - Soak your feet in epsom salt and you will relax after a long day or a long workout. I love soaking my feet and relaxing in a nice meditation.

25. **Ear plugs** - The best way to fall asleep or concentrate is to wear ear plugs. Keep them around the house for everyday use.

The key is to have the things that you need to be healthy around because if you have a healthy environment, you will end up being healthier.

Have a place where you do your workouts, a special cup that you use to hydrate and create rituals for yourself and your habits will take you to your goals automatically.

"Those who fail to prepare for high energy, might as well prepare to fail."
- Joe Apfelbaum

7 Books That Helped Me In My Journey

I was never a fan of reading books about health. I was way too focused on business and learning skills to earn a living.

If health is a priority to you, you must invest time into learning about your health and there is no better way than reading more books about health and productivity.

4 Hour Body - Tim Ferris
Tim did so much research in this book and it helped me learn so much. It's a really big book so feel free to skip around to the parts that interest you most.

10 Day Green Smoothie Cleanse - JJ Smith
I am a big fan of smoothies in general so when I learned about this best-selling book I got really excited. I love the part in the book where she explains things in a simple way that I can understand.

Fast Diet - Dr Michael Mosley
This book covers the science of fasting and how it helps people lose weight. It's a powerful book that helped me really change my levels of energy and not rely on food.

How Not to Die - Michael Greger M.D.
There are many myths about what works and what doesn't work. Michael breaks down the why and how of most major diseases and what you can do to stay healthy and high energy.

The Miracle Morning - Hal Elrod
When I wanted to start getting up earlier, I found Hal's book and it was a fantastic resource for me to get more energy by learning how to change my habits to wake up earlier.

The Mindbody Prescription - John Sarno M.D.
It's hard to feel high energy with you have back pain. John helps you understand how the mind is really what is causing the pain and how to eliminate back pain forever.

Getting Things Done - David Allen
The best way to get yourself to be healthy is to have a great plan and to execute. The problem is we have too many things to do and adding another thing to do will cause us stress. This system will help you get it all done and give you the energy to do more.

I can probably list another 300 books that you will get immense benefit from but I challenge you to not just read those 7 books but to study them so that you can put them into action in your life.

Start with ONE book at a time and read the next chapter to finish this book.

Which book will you get from this list?

Feel free to send me a message with the books that impacted you the most in your journey!

"Read books, change your thoughts. Change your thoughts, change your life."
- Joe Apfelbaum

How to Keep Up A Healthy Lifestyle Forever

People are living their life on a YO YO diet. One month they are healthy the next they are not and their energy levels are all over the place.

You want to find a place where you can maintain your energy and health for the rest of your life.

There are two things to keep in mind.

1. You will get bored of your routine so you have to keep mixing it up.
2. You have to learn the basics and create the habits that make the basics automatic.

Many people lose weight but they gain it right back. Many people make money but they have a hard time keeping it. The key to really succeeding is learning how to maintain your success when you get there.

Having the right awareness, the right strategy and keeping yourself accountable will make sure that you do not slip back into an unenergetic state.

Surround yourself with people who will encourage your high energy lifestyle and cheer you on to keep living the type of life that you strive to live.

Please stay in touch with me and let me know how I can support you on your journey. I am here to add value and to support you with your high energy goals!

Thank you for taking the time to read this book and I hope you found it useful.

Please share your comments with me via my website
www.joeapfelbaum.com. I would love to hear from you.

"Be yourself. You are a beautiful being that has the right to exist."

- Joe Apfelbaum

If you enjoyed this book, please let a friend know about it so they can benefit from this information too.

Send them to
www.highenergysecrets.com

The best thing you can do for someone you care about is buy them a book.

Knowledge is not power, Applied knowledge is power!

Take action today!

Stay Mojovated!

#Mojovation

- Joe Apfelbaum
www.joeapfelbaum.com

Want to learn more about Joe Apfelbaum?

Visit www.joeapfelbaum.com

You can listen to podcasts, read articles and find out how to get even more resources to grow yourself and your business.

Joe Apfelbaum is available for public speaking, coaching and consulting.

You can reach joe via email at joe@joeapfelbaum.com

Please share a link to www.highenergysecrets.com to let people know how this important project affected your life.